# Making a
# Difference:

## Putting Jewish Spirituality Into Action, One Mitzvah at a Time

## Teaching Guide by Diane A. Cohen

BEHRMAN HOUSE, INC.

# Table of Contents

*Editor:* Gila Gevirtz
*Production Manager:* Sheila Plotkin
*Design:* Imagination Ink
*Special Needs Education Consultant:* Sarah Rubinow Simon

Copyright © 2001 by Behrman House, Inc.
ISBN: 0-87441-713-9
www.behrmanhouse.com
Manufactured in the United States of America

# Introduction

*Making a Difference* is an important resource for Jewish educators and students. It offers a lively and motivating program for helping teens choose a personal ethic that solidifies their identities as Jews, and it is grounded in Jewish sources and actions that help make the world a better place.

The book speaks in teen-friendly language and presents Jewish wisdom and values in a way that is relevant to the lives and interests of American adolescents. It speaks to teens not as members of a "lost generation" but as the thinking, feeling, caring people they are.

— *David Yammer, Ph.D.*
   *School Psychologist,*
   *The Abraham Joshua Heschel School*

*Making a Difference* was written because Judaism has much to say about securing children's developing moral and spiritual foundations as they navigate through the challenges of adolescence. It connects teens' developing sense of responsibility and morality with the higher context of ethics and performing mitzvot.

Combining proven conceptual frameworks with engaging hands-on activities, each chapter of *Making a Difference* creates a perfect learning cycle. The more adolescents learn to give of themselves through mitzvot, the better they feel about themselves. The stronger their egos, the higher their self-esteem is built and the more they can understand and withstand the call of temptation in today's material world.

— *Paula Drill, M.S.W.*

*Making a Difference: Putting Jewish Spirituality Into Action, One Mitzvah at a Time* presents an action-based view of Jewish spirituality. The book discusses both ethical and ritual mitzvot and includes many practical and creative suggestions for how to observe them. Each chapter focuses on one mitzvah and includes the following activities:

- *Self-Portrait* Thinking about the mitzvah in personal terms

- *You Don't Say!* Finding modern meaning in the wisdom of our sages

- *It's a Dilemma!* Responding to provocative, real-life situations

- *Think About It!* Exploring probing questions that stimulate critical thinking

- *Mitzvah Journal* Recording personal experiences of observing the mitzvot

Like the textbook, this teaching guide is easy to use and adapt to your personal teaching style and strengths, and to your students' learning styles and interests. Every chapter in the textbook has a complementary chapter in the teaching guide, and each chapter in the teaching guide includes the following:

- *Learning Objectives* Statement of the chapter objectives

- *Chapter Overview* Brief summary of the chapter content

- *Key Words* Essential vocabulary with definitions

- *Teaching Opportunities*
   **Set Inductions** Practical suggestions for introducing the chapter
   **Techniques** Teaching tips, discussion ideas, and enrichment activities
   **Answer Keys** Where appropriate, answers to questions posed in the textbook

- *Family Activities* Sample letters to parents, and family activities that can extend classroom learning and keep parents informed about what is happening in class

Finally, there is a section (see page 48) that will guide you in adapting classroom activities to the requirements of students with special needs.

Together, the textbook and teaching guide provide you with a wide variety of discussion topics and activities. You may not have time for everything. Select the topics and activities that best suit you and your students, considering factors such as time constraints and interests, as well as your teaching skills and the strengths and needs of your students.

### BEFORE YOU BEGIN...

In the early stages of their religious education, your students developed basic Hebrew and prayer skills as well as a core knowledge of Jewish history, tradition, and values. Now, as preteens and teens, they increasingly will want to bring their personal experiences and insights to discussions of these subjects. *Making a Difference* will help them do so. Through a variety of activities that develop students' creative and critical thinking skills, the textbook helps students consider how Jewish tradition and values can play a part in their growing sense of self, their Jewish identification, and their independence.

As they work through *Making a Difference*, encourage your students to choose mitzvah projects that help them express who they are, what they believe in, and how that fits in with the commitments they will make as Jews. When they share their experiences and points of view, make it clear that your classroom is a safe place where they will be listened to with respect, guided rather than judged. And when students prefer not to share, respect their privacy, allowing them time for personal reflection without having to "go public."

## Say It In Hebrew

Listed below, in Hebrew and transliteration, are the names of the mitzvot that are presented in *Making a Difference*. When you introduce each chapter, you may want to write the name of the relevant mitzvah in Hebrew on the chalkboard and review it with your students. Encourage your students to use these Hebrew words during class discussions.

| TEXTBOOK PAGE | TEACHING GUIDE PAGE | MITZVAH | |
|:---:|:---:|---|---:|
| 17 | 10 | Tzedakah | צְדָקָה |
| 28 | 13 | Rodef Shalom | רוֹדֵף שָׁלוֹם |
| 40 | 17 | Shabbat | שַׁבָּת |
| 48 | 20 | Ahavat Tziyon | אַהֲבַת צִיּוֹן |
| 60 | 23 | Bal Tashḥit | בַּל תַּשְׁחִית |
| 68 | 26 | Kashrut | כַּשְׁרוּת |
| 78 | 29 | Sh'mirat Habriyut | שְׁמִירַת הַבְּרִיאוּת |
| 89 | 32 | Bikkur Ḥolim | בִּקוּר חוֹלִים |
| 99 | 35 | Kibbud Av Va'em | כִּבּוּד אָב וָאֵם |
| 111 | 38 | Sh'mirat Halashon | שְׁמִירַת הַלָּשׁוֹן |
| 119 | 41 | Tefillah | תְּפִלָּה |
| 130 | 44 | Talmud Torah | תַּלְמוּד תּוֹרָה |

# ① Getting Connected

Textbook pages 7–8

## LEARNING OBJECTIVES

Students will be able to:

- define mitzvot as sacred actions that connect us to God
- explain what they will learn about in *Making a Difference*

## CHAPTER OVERVIEW

This brief chapter introduces students to the notion that they have a choice: They can make the experience of being a bar or bat mitzvah a one-day affair or the beginning of a lifetime commitment. It explains that *Making a Difference* will help them become the adults they hope to be by learning to perform Jewish sacred acts—mitzvot.

## KEY WORDS

- *Brit:* agreement; covenant; a reference to the covenant between God and the Jewish people
- *Mitzvot:* commandments (from God)

## TEACHING OPPORTUNITIES

### SET INDUCTION

Hand out a textbook to each member of the class. Ask students to look at the cover—the title, subtitle, and images—and tell you what they think the book will be about. *(how to improve the world; movies about Jews; giving tzedakah; our relationship with God)*

*Note:* For information on Elijah's cup, turn to page 11 of *Making a Difference*; for information on the illustration of a woman, turn to page 42.

Now have your students turn to the Table of Contents on page 5 and ask them to read through the chapter titles and subtitles. Ask them what the titles of chapters 3 through 14 are *(mitzvot)* and which ones they recognize.

After giving your students a few minutes to browse through the book, draw a horizontal line, about

4 feet in length, on the board. At one end write "birth." Say: Imagine that this is the timeline of your life. Let's say that today, you are here *(make a mark about 6 inches from the birth point)*. You have many more years ahead of you. Does anyone know *exactly* what will happen in their lives over the course of the remaining years? *(Most students will indicate that at best they have some idea of what the possibilities are but don't know exactly what will happen.)* But do you have some plans for what you hope to do and achieve? *(graduate from high school and college or other post-high school training, succeed in building a career, find a loving partner, build a career, travel)*

Explain that an important part of growing up is to set goals and to dream dreams. Planning for the *kind* of adult we want to become is a critical part of the process. We may not be able to plan all the events in our lives, but we *can* build our own character through the daily choices we make, and these choices can help us become the adults we dream of being.

Invite students to name some of the character traits they hope will describe them when they are adults. Write these on the chalkboard. *(integrity, truthfulness, generosity, kindness, reliability, confidence, compassion)* Explain that they will now read the first chapter of *Making a Difference* to learn how the Jewish tradition can help them become the adults they dream of being.

Invite several volunteers to read chapter 1 aloud, asking each to read two or three paragraphs.

Ask: What does holy mean? *(special, sacred, different. You may add the notion that feeling holy means feeling connected to God.)*

### EXTRAORDINARY VS. SUPERHUMAN (page 8)

Ask: What do you think the authors meant by "The holiness of living as a bar or bat mitzvah can transform ordinary days into extraordinary days?" *(Performing mitzvot connects us to God, to something greater than ourselves, and thus makes each day more magnificent and meaningful.)*

# Taking Action

Textbook pages 9–16

## LEARNING OBJECTIVES

Students will be able to:

- differentiate between the concepts of ritual mitzvot and ethical mitzvot
- identify mitzvot they already perform and consider how these mitzvot affect their daily lives

## CHAPTER OVERVIEW

This chapter presents an overview of the Covenant (Brit) between the Jewish people and God and explains how the Torah, the books of the prophets, and the Talmud contribute to our understanding of the mitzvot and how to perform them. It defines ritual and ethical mitzvot and how they help us live as a holy people.

## KEY WORDS

- **Ethical Mitzvot:** mitzvot that define our relationship with God's creations (people, animals, the environment), for example, acts of generosity, showing compassion to pets, acting as a peacemaker
- **Ritual Mitzvot:** mitzvot that are concerned with our relationship with God and our personal identification with Judaism, for example, prayer and observing Shabbat

## TEACHING OPPORTUNITIES

### SET INDUCTION

Ask your students to describe moments when they have felt surrounded by holiness, or have felt a presence they thought of as God's. *(when they avoided a serious injury, saw a sunset, held a newborn baby, carried a Torah scroll)* Ask if they would like to have that feeling more often and how they think they could get it. *(spend more time outdoors, pray, study Torah)* Explain that in this chapter of *Making a Difference*, they will learn how to become more aware of God's presence in the world and find out how performing mitzvot can help them feel closer to God.

*Note:* If you or your students are uncomfortable talking about God, use alternative words, such as "godly," "godliness," "sacred," "holiness," or the Hebrew word *kadosh*, meaning "holy." You also may want to suggest that students use traditional names for God that embody qualities they associate with holiness, such as *Shalom* (Peace), *Hayotzer* (The Creator), and *Harahaman* (The Compassionate One).

### THE TEN COMMANDMENTS (page 10)

Read the second commandment and ask your students what they think idols are. *(false gods)* Ask for examples of modern idols—people or things that are treated as if they were holy. *(movie stars, sports heroes, money, cars)* Ask students how observing the second commandment can protect us from worshipping such idols. *(It can remind us that there is only one God; it can remind us that physical objects can be bought, sold, and traded and are not worthy of becoming the most important things in our lives.)*

### RITUAL AND ETHICAL MITZVOT (page 11)

Have students read the feature silently, or ask volunteers to read aloud. Invite your students to name mitzvot with which they are familiar. List their responses on the chalkboard, in two columns, with ritual mitzvot in one column and ethical mitzvot in the other. Don't put titles on the columns yet. If the students focus on ritual mitzvot, such as lighting Shabbat or Ḥanukkah candles, eating matzah on Passover, and observing kashrut, ask questions to encourage the citing of ethical mitzvot. *("Name mitzvot that teach us to treat others with kindness and justice."* gemilut ḥasadim *[acts of lovingkindness]*, rodef shalom *[pursuing justice])* If the students focus on ethical mitzvot, such as giving tzedakah, visiting the sick, honoring parents, and recycling), ask questions to encourage the listing of ritual mitzvot. *("Name a mitzvah you perform in synagogue."* tefillah *[prayer]*, talmud Torah *[studying Torah])*

Now ask students how they would label the columns *(Ethical Mitzvot and Ritual Mitzvot).*

### Enrichment

There are two ways to label these lists. One way is to label them as ritual mitzvot and ethical mitzvot. Another way is to call the ritual mitzvot *mitzvot bein adam lamakom*—mitzvot between people and God—and to call the ethical mitzvot *mitzvot bein adam l'havero*—mitzvot between one person and another.

### THE CHOICES YOU MAKE ARE IMPORTANT (page 13)

After students read and discuss the text on page 13, consider doing an art project. Have your students work in groups of two or three to create large posters out of butcher block paper that can be hung in your classroom or in the hallway of your school. The theme of each poster can be "Mitzvot Keep Us Connected." Here are some suggestions to help students think of the words and images they want to include: visiting the ill, bringing clothing to a shelter for the homeless, studying Torah as a group, giving a concert at an old-age home, praying in synagogue, or participating in the Torah service.

### TEENS MAKE A DIFFERENCE (page 14)

Working individually, in small groups, or as a class, have your students describe some of the character traits Mark Guterman might have developed in himself to be able to create Operation Sports Stuff. *(initiative, ability to work hard, patience, generosity, caring, persistence, organization)* Then, as a class, discuss whether or not, your students think Mark is an extraordinary person to have accomplished what he has. Ask them to explain their answers.

### YOU DON'T SAY! (page 15)

Encourage your students to think back on a time when they were tempted to do something they knew they shouldn't. *(Examples might include a classmate offering them a cigarette, drugs, or alcohol, the temptation to cheat on a test, or lying because they were afraid of getting into trouble if they told the truth.)* What made them stop? *(something their parents said; something they learned in religious school; fear of possible consequences)*

# Family Activity

Compose a letter to the parents of your students in which you explain what your class has been studying and suggest a family activity to reinforce the lesson. Below is a sample letter.

---

Dear Parent:

Our class has just studied the two categories of mitzvot (sacred actions, or commandments): ritual mitzvot, such as observing Shabbat and praying, and ethical mitzvot, such as pursuing peace and justice. We have learned that both are important in Jewish life.

To reinforce what we have studied, you and your child may want to participate in the following family activity. Make a list of the mitzvot that are already a part of your family life. For example, perhaps you light Shabbat candles, contribute tzedakah, participate in Passover seders, treat one another with respect, and visit the sick. After you make your list, discuss how these mitzvot enrich your lives and keep you connected to something larger than your individual selves or family—for example, to the Jewish community, to past generations, to Israel, and to God.

Please encourage your child to share with our class some of the examples of how observing mitzvot has had an impact on your lives.

Sincerely,

[Your name]

# ③ Tzedakah

## giving justly

Textbook pages 17–27

### LEARNING OBJECTIVES

Students will be able to:

- differentiate between tzedakah and charity
- articulate a connection between giving tzedakah and bringing justice to the world
- identify ways to contribute tzedakah that are personally and communally meaningful

### CHAPTER OVERVIEW

This chapter distinguishes between *charity*, a voluntary act of generosity, and *tzedakah*, the mitzvah that obligates Jews to give to those in need. Judaism teaches that sharing one's resources and talents with those in need is a form of pursuing justice, and that even the poor are obligated to give tzedakah. Students are presented with a variety of practical tzedakah projects.

### KEY WORD

***Tzedakah:*** sharing one's resources, such as money, food, time, and talents, with those who are in need

### SET INDUCTION

Ask your class: Has a stranger ever asked you for money for food? How did it feel? *(good, not good, scary)* What did you do? *(disregarded the person, gave him some money, bought her a sand-wich)* Ask: To what, if anything, would you feel obligated to contribute time, money, or other resources? *(food and clothing drive, hospital fund-raiser, animal shelter, the synagogue)* Ask them why they do or don't feel obligated to give. Then tell them that this chapter of *Making a Difference* will teach them about the Jewish value of tzedakah and how it differs from charity.

## CHARITY VS. TZEDAKAH (page 18)

Role-play: To assign roles prepare one slip of paper per student. On the first four write one of each of the following:

1. Poor person
2. Wealthy person
3. Teenager
4. Person who has just lost his or her job

On the remaining slips write "Tzedakah Committee."

Put the slips of paper in a paper bag and pass the bag around, asking each student to take a slip. Those students on the Tzedakah Committee will form a group and approach the other four students, one at a time, for the following role-play. (If you have a large class, you might increase the number of characters beyond four to include an overworked business person and a visitor to the synagogue.)

Before beginning the role-play, ask the class to brainstorm several projects for which the Tzedakah Committee might need help, such as a clothing drive, a phonathon, and an interfaith Thanksgiving dinner for the needy. Then have the committee members approach the characters, one at a time, to discuss the projects and how they can assist.

Help your students consider what each person could offer. (*time—making phone calls, making a financial contribution, donating used clothing*)

## GETTING TO THE ROOT (page 18)

How can helping those in need add justice to the world? (*It is not fair that some people live in parts of the world that have strong economies while others live in poverty-stricken areas with frequent natural disasters, such as droughts and earthquakes. Similarly, it is not fair that some people live long and healthy lives and others suffer from disabling illnesses and diseases. Tzedakah adds justice by creating more of a balance between those who have and those who need.*)

## THINK ABOUT IT! (page 18)

Ask your students to consider how helping others can add to one's dignity. (*helps the person see that he or she has something to give*)

## REACH OUT AND HELP SOMEONE (page 19)

Discuss the Jewish tradition of donating money in memory of a loved one and to celebrate joyous life-cycle events. Then ask students to bring in newsletters from a variety of Jewish institutions and organizations, such as the synagogue, local Jewish community center, Hadassah, and New Israel Fund. (You might bring some newsletters to class as backup.) Ask the students to find the donations page in each newsletter and identify reasons people contribute to the organizations (*in honor of a baby naming, wedding, or anniversary*)

## DID YOU KNOW? (page 19)

(*One reason people who are poor may give more is that they understand from personal experience how important help is and thus are more willing to help others.*)

## LEVELS OF TZEDAKAH (page 20)

Organize the students in groups of two or three and ask them to do the exercise "Levels of Tzedakah." As a class, discuss the responses to the questions.

## CREATING A BALANCE (page 20)

Applying Hillel's philosophy to your own life:
1. *Doing something for yourself might mean taking a break when you are tired; reading or listening to music; exercising to work off stress.*
2. *Helping others might mean working in a soup kitchen; volunteering at a local hospital or senior center.*

3. *If not now, when? People need our help now! And as for "doing something for yourself," when we need to take care of ourselves, we can't put it off. If we spend all our time helping others, we wear ourselves out and can't help anyone.*

### HOW SHOULD TZEDAKAH BE GIVEN (page 21)

Brainstorm as a class some of the needs people have. How might society fill those needs in a way that preserves people's dignity? *(Rather than giving used clothes directly to the poor, have those in need purchase the clothes for a modest amount from a thrift store; have those in need help prepare and serve the meals in a soup kitchen.)*

### YOU DON'T SAY! (page 21)

*(God speaks through the acts of lovingkindness that are performed by human beings. When a person gives tzedakah or performs other acts of kindness, it is as if God is speaking.)*

### READY! SET! GO! (pages 22–24)

Have your students read and discuss the descriptions of the tzedakah projects, then have them work on one or several projects individually, in small groups, or as a class. Alternatively, students may use the projects in *Making a Difference* as springboards for developing their own ideas.

*Note:* There is a "Resources" section on pages 141–42 of the textbook which may be helpful to your students as they plan their projects. They may also add to the list of resources as they do their own research.

### TEENS MAKE A DIFFERENCE (page 25)

For a tzedakah project, you may want to take up a collection to buy a copy of *Come Cook with Me*, have the students prepare some of Madeline's recipes, and sell the food as a fund-raiser.

### IT'S A DILEMMA! (page 25)

Have students read and work through this activity individually, in small collaborative learning groups, or as a class. Help them acknowledge their discomfort if that is what they express. Discuss a variety of concerns and solutions, such as concerns for safety and the possibility of buying the person food.

### SELF-PORTRAIT (page 26)

Remember, the main purpose of this activity is to help students consider how Jewish tradition and values can play a part in their growing sense of self and independence. Permit them to share what they have written, but respect their desire for privacy if that is what they choose.

### MITZVAH JOURNAL (page 27)

Students can complete their journals at home or in class and can then participate in a class discussion. Encourage them to be honest in their responses, and set a tone of tolerance that makes being honest feel safe.

## Family Activity

As an alternative to sending a letter home offering suggestions for family activities devoted to tzedakah, you may want to invite your students and their families to participate in a school or synagogue tzedakah project, such as a food or clothing drive.

# Rodef Shalom

## peacemaking

Textbook pages 28–39

### LEARNING OBJECTIVES

Students will be able to:

- understand the importance Judaism places on pursuing peace
- perform acts that nurture peace within themselves, their families, and the broader community

### CHAPTER OVERVIEW

This chapter presents the many ways Judaism stresses the importance of pursuing peace—for example, through prayers, sacred texts, and symbols, such as the olive branches on the seal of Israel. It also provides students with practical ways in which they can develop greater personal calm, work to develop tolerance and *sh'lom bayit* (peace in the home), and contribute to making their community and the larger world a more harmonious and peaceful place.

### KEY WORDS

- *Shalom:* wholeness, completeness; peace; hello; goodbye
- *Sh'lom bayit:* peace in the home

### TEACHING OPPORTUNITIES

#### SET INDUCTION

You may want to introduce this mitzvah by showing a video of a feature film that can stimulate discussion about the importance of peace. It can be a movie that deals with concepts of war and peace, or a movie that looks at family relationships, such as *The Winslow Boy* (Sony Picture Classics, G-rated video).

After viewing the movie, have your students discuss the feelings and thoughts it evoked and share what their own experience has been with conflict and peacemaking. Then tell them that in this chapter of *Making a Difference* they will explore how Judaism helps us bring greater peace to our own lives and to the larger world.

### HEARING THE STILL, SMALL VOICE (page 29)

Have students respond to the questions in writing, then share their responses in class if they choose. How would you describe the voice in your heart? *(quiet; calm; soft; gentle; kind)* How do you keep in touch with it? *(close my eyes and sit quietly, pray silently, participate in synagogue services, read poetry, meditate)*

### YOU DON'T SAY! (page 29)

Invite a student to lead a class discussion based on this activity. *(The Torah teaches justice and respect for other people and other creations including the disabled, the poor, widows, orphans, animals, and the environment. When we observe the mitzvot, we help create a more fair and peaceful world.)*

### Photograph of Seal of the State of Israel (page 30)

Note: The seal of the State of Israel depicts a menorah similar to those that stood in the ancient Temple in Jerusalem. At the bottom of the emblem is the word *Yisrael*, "Israel" in Hebrew.

### THINK ABOUT IT! (page 31)

Divide your class into collaborative learning groups of two or three students and ask them to discuss the questions in the box for 5 to 10 minutes. Then have them reconvene as a class to share their ideas. Note that the text refers to "unnecessary arguments." Ask for examples of unnecessary arguments. *(arguing with a sibling about who cleaned up more or helped less; arguing with a parent about lowering the volume of your music when you know you've been inconsiderate)*

How else can you prepare to become a peacemaker? *(listen carefully to what others say, not shout back when someone shouts at you)* How can pursuing peace help you become a responsible citizen and Jew? *(When you become used to thinking as part of a community, you begin to think about how to seek the welfare of that community, to make compromises and accommodations.)*

### SHALOM—THE HEART AND SOUL OF JUDAISM (page 31)

Have students read the text silently or invite one student to the front of the class to read it aloud. Then tell this story of the *Kohen Gadol* (High Priest): The Midrash records that Aaron, Moses' brother and the High Priest, knew of two men whose anger kept them apart. He went to one man and said, "Your friend is upset about the anger that distances you. He wants to make amends." Then he went to the other man and said the same thing. He convinced each that the other wanted to begin the conversation to heal their rift. In this way he brought them together.

Discuss the story and ask: What problem might there be with Aaron's peacemaking tactics? *(lying)* What does this story teach us about Judaism's views on peace and truth? *(Judaism places a high value on peace, permitting one to lie for the sake of maintaining or creating peace.)*

### READY! SET! GO! (pages 32–33, 36–37)

As a class, read and discuss the suggestions for fulfilling the mitzvah of *rodef shalom*. Then have your students work individually, in small groups, or as a class on developing their skills in working as peacemakers. Alternatively, they may use the ideas in *Making a Difference* as springboards for developing their own projects.

### Photograph of Civil Rights March (page 36)

When asked about this march, Rabbi Heschel said that he was praying with his feet. What do you think he meant? (You may want to compare this activity with the "You Don't Say!" activity on page 21 of the textbook—see page 12 of this teaching guide.)

**Photograph of Video Game** (page 36)

This role-playing activity is set in a courtroom. Assign the following roles (the number of characters will depend on the size of your class): one judge or two to three members of a jury, a plaintiff, a defendant, a prosecutor, a defense lawyer, and witnesses—for example, a school psychologist or social worker, rabbi, representative of the company that manufactures the game, classmates of the plaintiff.

*The Case:* The plaintiff, who is accused of disrupting classes, making noise, and pushing people around, has been suspended from school. He or she is suing the defendant, a designer of a computer game called *Trash the School*, claiming that the game made the plaintiff behave in ways that threaten his or her ability to function in school. The defendant claims, "It's just a game."

Both sides should make opening arguments, examine and cross-examine the witnesses, then make closing statements. Then the judge or jury should make and pronounce a decision.

**SENSE OR CENSORSHIP?** (page 37)

Ask for volunteers to debate the following resolution: Be it resolved that restrictions on access to TV and the Internet for teens are an illegal form of censorship. Have the volunteers form two groups—one anti and one pro. Hold a 10- to 15-minute debate and then have the class vote on the resolution. If your students vote in favor of the resolution, do a role playing activity or lead a class discussion that helps them consider the possible consequences of the resolution.

**SELF-PORTRAIT** (page 34)

Suggest that students share their ideas on positive ways to handle stress. *(exercising, talking with a caring adult or friend, considering what might be eliminated from their schedule to relieve a time pressure)*

**IT'S A DILEMMA!** (page 35)

Have students read and work through this activity individually, in small collaborative learning groups, or as a class. Before they respond to the dilemma, encourage them to think about the strategies they have read about in the chapter: listening patiently to others, speaking respectfully to those with whom they have disagreements, remaining calm, and weighing their own point of view against the value of the relationship.

**YOU DON'T SAY!** (page 35)

Keep in mind that many students live in homes where there are stresses and conflicts that are outside their control. Therefore, it is important to acknowledge that while each person can contribute to making a home *more* peaceful, no one person can make a home *completely* peaceful.

If a student expresses concern about the specifics of conflict in his or her home, suggest that you discuss it after class. You may also want to consult with the educational director or rabbi. To the extent that someone chooses to discuss something personal in class, remind your students that their classroom should be a safe place to share, free from gossip and judgment.

**YOU DON'T SAY!** (page 38)

What does it mean that one makes peace with one's enemy? Does this mean we never argue with friends? Of course not! But in friendship there is an underlying agreement to compromise and consider the other person's feelings and perspectives. But when we think of someone as our enemy, we can be tempted to become inflexible, defensive, or even offensive.

**MITZVAH JOURNAL** (page 39)

Students can complete their journals at home or in class and then participate in a class discussion.

# Family Activity

Here is a sample letter.

---

Dear Parent:

Our class has been studying the mitzvah of *rodef shalom*, pursuing peace—within oneself, the family, the community, and the larger world. We have discussed the importance Jewish tradition places on achieving peace and we have considered strategies for pursuing peace.

Shabbat is a day that is especially dedicated to peace. This Friday night or at lunch on Saturday, consider asking your child to share with you some of the strategies he or she learned in class for peacemaking. You may then want to discuss how these strategies can be used to strengthen your family ties.

Sincerely,

[Your name]

# ⑤ Shabbat

## an extraordinary day

Textbook pages 40–47

## LEARNING OBJECTIVES

Students will be able to:

- articulate how observing Shabbat can enrich their lives
- apply the concept of *menuḥah*, or rest, to their observance of Shabbat
- list a variety of ways to observe Shabbat that are both pleasurable and meaningful to them

## KEY WORDS

- *Menuḥah:* rest
- *Shabbat:* the seventh day of the week; a sacred day

## CHAPTER OVERVIEW

This chapter helps students understand Shabbat as a gift, a day that frees us from workday obligations and enables us to find holiness in our relationships with God, the people we love, and the rest of Creation. It presents a variety of ways in which students can become more committed to Shabbat observance and enjoy the beauty of the day.

## TEACHING OPPORTUNITIES

### SET INDUCTION

Bring two Shabbat candles and candlesticks with matches to class. Before your students enter your classroom, turn off the lights, lower the shades, and light the Shabbat candles. On the chalkboard write the following instructions: (1) please sit quietly in your seat; (2) relax your body and mind by closing your eyes or focusing on the candles; (3) breathe in deeply and exhale slowly. As students enter, motion them to sit down quietly and point to the chalkboard. (If you feel comfortable doing so, you can lead a guided meditation in which students imagine themselves on a sunny, peaceful, lush island— Shabbat is sometimes referred to as "an island in time.")

After a few minutes, in a gentle voice, tell your students that you are about to turn on the lights. Ask them to describe the difference between how the class began today and how it usually begins. Have them describe how they felt today in contrast to how they usually feel. Guide the conversation into the usefulness of feeling relaxed and restful as well as being active and productive. Then explain that Judaism respects both. Tell your students that they will be learning more about this idea in the next chapter of *Making a Difference*.

### A GIFT AND A CHOICE: ART/WRITING PROJECT (pages 40-41)

Distribute paper to the students and ask them to draw or write a poem or essay that describes Shabbat as a gift or a palace in time.

### SELF-PORTRAIT (page 41)

Ask for volunteers to share their responses. Encourage students to try to describe why the time they spend in these contexts makes time feel holy.

### READY! SET! GO! (pages 42–45)

As a class, read and discuss the suggestions for fulfilling the mitzvah of observing Shabbat, then ask each student to select one or several of the suggestions that are personally meaningful. To help your students make their choices, you can organize the following activity.

Divide the class into seven groups and have each group research one suggestion. For example, the group that is assigned "Make Your Friday Night Meal Special" could teach the class to sing "Shalom Aleichem" and recite Kiddush and Hamotzi. They might also teach one or two Shabbat *z'mirot*, or songs; you can provide them with copies of the

words in Hebrew and English to distribute to the class. Also consider bringing in objects associated with performing various Shabbat rituals mentioned on these pages, such as candles and candlesticks, a Kiddush cup, ḥallah cover, two ḥallot, and a *Havdalah* set.

There needn't be an equal number of students in each group. In a small class, the groups can research more than one suggestion. Assign the number of students on the basis of how complex the task is.

### IT'S A DILEMMA! (page 45)

Have the students read the text silently. Then elicit from them the realities of Shabbat in their lives: What do they really do on Friday nights and Saturdays? What pressures do they feel? How might observing Shabbat decrease the pressures? How could becoming active in the synagogue community or a Jewish youth group help them become more observant of Shabbat?

### THE FREEDOM TO OBSERVE MITZVOT (page 46)

What other mitzvot can be observed only by free people? Why? *(kashrut [Jewish dietary laws]— oppressed or enslaved people often have little or no control over the food that is available to them; Torah study—oppressed or enslaved people often don't have the time or freedom to study what they choose)*

### MITZVAH JOURNAL (page 47)

Students can complete their journals at home or in class and then participate in a class discussion.

# Family Activity

Here is a sample letter.

---

Dear Parent:

We have just completed a unit on Shabbat. Ask your child to share what was discussed in class regarding the value and rituals of observing Shabbat.

If you do not currently observe Shabbat but want to begin, or if you want to extend your observance, ask your child for suggestions. In addition, if you do not already attend synagogue services on Shabbat, you might consider joining us on Friday night or Saturday morning in order to become better acquainted with our community and to discover opportunities to learn more about Shabbat observance.

Sincerely,

[Your name]

# ⑥ Ahavat Tziyon

## for the love of Israel

Textbook pages 48–59

## LEARNING OBJECTIVES

Students will be able to:

- identify Israel as the Jewish homeland
- articulate a vision of Israel as a "light unto the nations"
- perform acts of *ahavat Tziyon*, love of Israel, that have personal meaning for them

## KEY WORDS

- **Ahavat Tziyon:** love of Zion, or Israel
- **Medinat Yisrael:** the modern state of Israel
- **Tziyon:** a hill in Jerusalem; also, the entire city; also, the Land of Israel

## CHAPTER OVERVIEW

This chapter presents a brief history of the Jews' ties to the Land of Israel and of Zionism. It describes many facets of modern life in Israel and helps students understand how they can build their own ties to the Jewish homeland.

## TEACHING OPPORTUNITIES

### SET INDUCTION

Begin the class by handing out the words to "Hatikvah" in both Hebrew and English. Explain that *hatikvah* means "the hope." Read the lyrics in English and ask your students what they know from the Bible and Jewish history that helps them understand why for almost two thousand years Jews yearned to return to Zion (the Land of Israel)? *(It is the homeland of the Jewish people; it is where our matriarchs and patriarchs lived; it is where the Holy Temple stood; Jews were oppressed in many lands; Jerusalem is considered by Jews as the holiest place in the world.)*

Review the lyrics in Hebrew with the class, then ask your students to stand, and either lead them in the singing of "Hatikvah" or invite your cantor or music teacher to do so.

Tell your students that in this chapter of *Making a Difference* they will learn about the importance of Israel to the Jewish people and to our vision of a better world.

### SELF-PORTRAIT (page 49)

Help your students understand that at the core of being a Jew is the willingness to struggle with difficult issues and relationships. Judaism *doesn't* require that we be perfect or that we always have faith; it *does* require that we make an effort to overcome difficulties to improve ourselves. It requires that we reach out to ask for help, and to help others.

### THE PROMISE OF THE HOLY LAND (page 50)

You may want to give a copy of your synagogue's *humash* to each student and invite volunteers to read aloud selections from the Bible that focus on our ancestors' experience in the Land of Israel. For example, they might read from Genesis 13, in which God establishes the Covenant with Abraham and sends him to the Land of Canaan (the ancient name of Israel).

### YOU DON'T SAY! (page 51)

Invite a student to the front of the class to read the text. Then ask the class, "What does it mean to will something?" *(to want to do something so strongly you put all your energy into it)* Examples of what students have willed and how they succeeded might include the following: *winning a sports or music competition by working hard and practicing regularly; making honor roll by studying diligently; improving a personal relationship by being more thoughtful.*

### IT'S A DILEMMA! (page 52)

Ask for volunteers to debate this resolution: Be it resolved that Israel should require all Jews to observe Shabbat when in public places in Israel. (This could mean that government offices would be closed, along with stores and movie theaters, and that no Jews would be permitted to operate a bus or taxi.) Hold a 10- to 15-minute debate and then have the class vote on the resolution.

### THINK ABOUT IT! (page 52)

Encourage students to respond honestly. As with most other issues, if students are permitted to be candid, they are more likely to remain open to different views. Thus, if you have students who do not feel connected to Israel or who believe that a connection to Israel is not vital to living a full Jewish life, permit them to speak freely and encourage other students to voice differing opinions and experiences.

### A LIGHT UNTO THE NATIONS (page 53)

How do the actions described in this feature show that modern Israel strives to be a light to other nations? *(Even though Israel is a small and young nation, it extends itself to those who are in need, fulfilling the obligation described in the Torah to care for the poor and the homeless.)* What impact do these actions have on the students? *(feel pride in Israel and in being a member of the Jewish people)* Would it be acceptable for Israel to be like every other nation? *(**Yes**: Israelis are just human beings. **No**: Israel is a Jewish state and therefore has an obligation to teach the lessons of Torah to the world.)*

### READY! SET! GO! (pages 54–58)

As a class, read and discuss the choices on these pages. Ask students to consider which suggestions are most practical and interesting. (Point out that the leading Israeli newspapers are available on-line.) If your school has an Internet connection, you may choose to bookmark those locations. Otherwise, you may share the locations with your students for home use. You may want to invite an older teen who has spent time in Israel to make a presentation to your class.

Ask your students to think about which suggestions they can add to their weekly or monthly routines and which would be better as occasional activities for them. Invite them to choose one or more suggestions to implement.

**SELF-PORTRAIT** (page 58)

Have the students complete the activity and share their responses with the class.

**MITZVAH JOURNAL** (page 59)

Students can complete their journals at home or in class and then participate in a class discussion.

## Family Activity

As a change of pace, rather than sending a letter home, you may want to invite your students' families to visit the class, perhaps on a Sunday morning. If any of the students or their family members has visited or lived in Israel, invite them to speak about their experiences and to show slides, photos, or videos of Israel. If none of your students or their family members have been to Israel, invite your rabbi, cantor, or another guest speaker to talk about the experiences he or she had in Israel.

If your synagogue has a gift shop, ask the person in charge to display items made in Israel. In addition, you might invite families who own Israeli-made objects, such as Kiddush cups or artwork, to bring them in for display.

# (7) Bal Tashhit

## every day is earth day

Textbook pages 60–67

### LEARNING OBJECTIVES

Students will be able to:

- discuss the significance of conservation as a mitzvah
- identify and perform acts of *bal tashhit*

### KEY WORD

*Bal Tashhit:* literally, do not destroy; conserving the resources of Creation—God's world, nature

### CHAPTER OVERVIEW

This chapter focuses on conservation not just as an act of social conscience, but as a sacred act, *bal tashhit*. Students are encouraged to develop the habit of performing acts of *bal tashhit*, such as recycling and conserving water and energy, as well as performing ritual mitzvot, such as reciting blessings that express gratitude for the wonders of nature. They are presented with a variety of practical measures they can take.

### TEACHING OPPORTUNITIES

#### SET INDUCTION

Read to the class the following midrash (a rabbinic story that illuminates the teachings of the Torah): God led Adam through the Garden of Eden and said, "I created all My beautiful and glorious works for your sake. Take care not to corrupt and destroy My world. For if you corrupt it, there is no one to make it right after you."

Ask: What does this midrash teach us? *(God expects people to be partners in caring for the world.)* Explain to your students that in this chapter of *Making a Difference* they will learn about the Jewish tradition of caring for the natural world.

## WE ARE CARETAKERS (page 60)

To stimulate a discussion on what it means to be caretakers of Creation—God's world, nature—ask the students if it is possible to own a piece of property in the legal sense but be a caretaker in the spiritual sense. (Have students explain their answers.) Ask them to describe how they can show mastery of the earth by using their talents to enrich and sustain life. (*plant and weed a garden, feed pets, recycle*)

## CONSERVATION IS AN ANCIENT JEWISH TRADITION (page 61)

Invite volunteers to read the text aloud. Ask students what they could change in the way they live that would help them become better caretakers of Creation. (*use scrap paper, wait until the dishwasher is filled with dirty dishes before running it, join an environmental group and/or contribute tzedakah to one*)

## IT'S A TRADITION (page 62)

Ask: How can reciting these blessings remind you that conservation is a Jewish tradition and a mitzvah? (*They can remind us that we are caretakers of God's world and that our tradition teaches us to nurture Creation's goodness.*)

## THINK ABOUT IT! (page 62)

Ask: Do you think that observing the mitzvah of *bal tashhit* is important enough to make it a part of your routine on a daily, weekly, or monthly basis? Why or why not?

## IT'S A DILEMMA! (page 63)

Have students read and work through this activity individually, in small collaborative learning groups, or as a class. (*Possible answers include: explain that you would like to recycle whatever materials their area collects; keep quiet so as not to offend the host; avoid using items, such as soda cans or paper plates, that you would normally recycle—offer to do the dishes instead.*)

## PLANET EARTH IS OUR EVERYDAY CONCERN (page 63)

What can you do on a daily basis? Arrange students in groups of two or three and ask them to brainstorm ideas. Share the responses as a class.

## READY! SET! GO! (pages 64–65)

Invite a speaker from COEJL (see the resource list on page 141 of *Making a Difference*) or another conservation group to speak to the class. Ask for printed materials in advance and have the students prepare questions for your guest regarding how they can observe the mitzvah of *bal tashhit* in school and at home.

## MAKING A DIFFERENCE (page 66)

Invite volunteers to read the text aloud. Ask your students how they can make a difference by observing the mitzvah of *bal tashhit* as individuals. As a class. As a synagogue community. Brainstorm one or more projects to undertake.

## YOU DON'T SAY! (page 66)

As a class or in small groups have your students brainstorm how they can remind themselves to protect and care for nature's gifts on a daily basis. (*Create posters, signs, photographs, bracelets, pendants.*) Have students brainstorm strategies for making these reminders. For example, those who want jewelry might make green beaded bracelets or pendants with a green Magen David (Jewish star). You may want to limit final choices to projects that can be done in the classroom.

## MITZVAH JOURNAL (page 67)

Students can complete their journals at home or in class and then participate in a class discussion.

# Family Activity

Here is a sample letter you might send home with your students.

Dear Parent:

Our class has just finished a unit on the Jewish value of *bal tashḥit*, conservation. After discussing the Jewish teaching that people are the caretakers of God's earth, we explored how the mitzvah of *bal tashḥit* teaches us to enhance nature and care for the wealth of natural resources we have been given.

Please help your child observe the mitzvah of *bal tashḥit* as part of daily life. As a family, spend a week paying close attention to your daily habits in regard to conservation—your use of water, Styrofoam cups, electricity, gasoline, etc. Consider specific changes you can make to conserve natural resources. Consider how observing the mitzvah of *bal tashḥit* can enrich your spiritual and personal connection to Judaism.

Please encourage your child to share your family's findings with our class.

Sincerely,

[Your name]

# ⑧ Kashrut

## you are what you eat

Textbook pages 68–77

### LEARNING OBJECTIVES

Students will be able to:

- explain the central principles of Jewish dietary laws
- demonstrate a working knowledge of the laws in terms of observance either for themselves or for guests in their home

### KEY WORDS

- **Kashrut:** fitness for use or consumption according to Jewish dietary laws
- **Pareve:** containing neither meat nor dairy; examples are fruit and vegetables
- **Shehitah:** Jewish ritual slaughter
- **Simhat Mitzvah:** joy of the commandment
- **Treif:** nonkosher
- **Tza'ar Ba'alei Hayyim:** compassion for animals

### CHAPTER OVERVIEW

This chapter focuses on how keeping kosher can remind us to honor our relationship with God, respect the sacredness of life, and reinforce our Jewish identification. Through the mitzvah of kashrut, every time we reach for something to eat, we have the opportunity to add holiness to our lives and remind ourselves of our Jewish heritage and observance. The chapter outlines the tenets of Jewish dietary laws and provides practical suggestions for observance.

### TEACHING OPPORTUNITIES

#### SET INDUCTION

Bring in five or six types of packaged foods. Try to include some with unexpected ingredients, such as soups that contain meat or milk products or have high amounts of fat, sugar, or salt, or even ingredients that some people may be allergic to, such as peanuts. One at a time, hold up the items and ask your students to name the ingredients they think are in them. List their responses on the chalkboard.

Have a volunteer read the ingredients listed on the packages and compare that list with what the students have guessed. Note the "surprise ingredients" and ask students why it might be a problem to buy products that have surprises in them. *(you may be allergic to the ingredient; it may have more fat than you want to eat; a family member might be on a low-salt diet; it may have too much sugar for a diabetic)* Explain that in this chapter of *Making a Difference* they will explore why Jewish law requires us to be concerned about the foods we eat—how they are prepared, what ingredients are in them, and what we eat with them.

## THE DIETARY LAWS (pages 69, 71)

You may want to invite your rabbi to present this section of the chapter. The rabbi can present the tradition as well as the synagogue's point of view on kashrut.

## THINK ABOUT IT! (page 69)

Ask your students: "What does, 'We are what we eat' mean?" *(Eating healthfully makes us stronger; eating junk food weakens us.)* What might the implications be of "You are what you eat" in terms of kashrut? *(Eating kosher food strengthens our Jewish identity.)* Ask your students if they think that American Jews' identities and values can be strengthened by keeping kosher. *(Often when we eat in kosher or vegetarian restaurants we find ourselves among other Jews; eating kosher food can remind us of the principle of choosing carefully and of making eating a sacred act; keeping kosher requires that we stop and make conscious choices before we eat; thinking before taking an action is a habit Judaism encourages us to cultivate.)*

Now ask your students if they think it is important to be able to eat the food served in any Jewish home or synagogue. *(**Yes:** Providing kosher food for guests at home or in a synagogue is a way of building community and making guests feel welcome. **No:** Different communities have different standards of kashrut and uniformity would be difficult to achieve.)*

## SELF-PORTRAIT (page 70)

Invite students to share their responses, but remember that the main purpose of this activity is to help students consider how Jewish tradition and values can play a part in their growing sense of self and independence. Permit them to share what they have written, but respect their desire for privacy, if that is what they choose.

## READY! SET! GO! (pages 72–73, 76)

As a class, read and discuss the text. Ask the students to consider which suggestions are most practical and motivating for them to implement. Also discuss the importance of being respectful of different choices that other family members may make. You can encourage a dialogue between students who currently observe kashrut and those who do not. You can also invite students who are vegetarian or who observe other dietary restrictions to share their experience.

You may want to invite a local kosher butcher to speak with your class and answer their questions.

## THINK ABOUT IT! (page 74)

After discussing the compassionate values of kashrut in relationship to animals, you may want to tell your students that many people (Jews and non-Jews) refused to buy lettuce and table grapes that were grown in California in the 1960s and 1970s in order to protest the inhumane treatment of migrant workers who harvested these crops. Ask your students if they think that lettuce and grapes that come from such farms should be considered unkosher? Ask if there are other foods they think should be considered unkosher because of issues of oppression or injustice. Ask if they think that physically damaging substances, such as cigarettes, should be considered unkosher.

## IT'S A DILEMMA! (page 75)

Organize this activity as a freeze-frame script: Ask for four or five volunteers to play the parts of friends, one of whom wants to keep kosher. Invite the rest of the class to gather around this group. Read aloud the scenario for this activity and ask the actors to begin improvising a conversation.

At each point where the friend who wants to keep kosher needs to make a decision, freeze the action and ask the class for input. Have the student who wants to keep kosher respond on the basis of the suggestions that have been made. Then freeze the action again to allow the class to give suggestions on how the friends might respond. Allow the dilemma to play itself out, then ask everyone—the actors and the other students—how it felt to make the decisions. Ask the actors who were the friends whether they thought of themselves as Jewish in the scene, and how their responses were affected.

## MITZVAH JOURNAL (page 77)

Students can complete their journals at home or in class and then participate in a class discussion.

---

## Family Activity

In place of a letter home, you may want to invite your students and their families to a special session on transforming mealtime into holy time through the foods we eat and the blessings we recite. Such a session might also include a discussion of the preciousness of eating together as a family, especially on Friday night. You may want to invite your rabbi to lead this session and present it as a schoolwide event.

---

# ⑨ Sh'mirat Habriyut

## be your best friend

Textbook pages 78–88

### LEARNING OBJECTIVES

Students will be able to:

- articulate the importance of caring for themselves as a mitzvah
- develop strategies for caring for their physical and emotional health

### KEY WORD

*Sh'mirat Habriyut:* caring for one's health

### CHAPTER OVERVIEW

This chapter presents the responsibility to care for one's self physically and emotionally as a mitzvah, a sacred act—*sh'mirat habriyut.* It grounds healthful habits—such as eating a nutritionally sound diet, exercising, and learning to cope with stress—in Jewish values and texts, and it provides practical suggestions for fulfilling the mitzvah.

*Note:* This chapter may touch on sensitive issues for some of your students—for example, their weight or eating habits, stress in their lives, and having their emotional needs met. Therefore, it will be particularly important that you provide a nonjudgmental learning environment in which students can choose to share or simply listen. If difficult issues arise, you may want to consult your educational director or rabbi.

### SET INDUCTION

Hang seven to ten large magazine pictures of people taking care of their physical and/or emotional health. For example, you might include a person taking vitamins; someone in a dentist's chair; someone being examined by a doctor; teens swimming, playing a sport, or exercising; people wearing seat belts in a car; someone sleeping; and someone talking to a rabbi.

Ask your students, "What makes all these pictures 'Jewish'?" Allow speculation, then say, "In each case one or more people are performing a mitzvah. Look again and see whether you can figure out what that mitzvah is."

After more speculation, explain that in each picture, someone is taking care of his or her physical and/or emotional well-being, and that is the mitzvah of *sh'mirat habriyut.* Tell your students that Judaism requires us not only to show respect for others but also to respect ourselves by taking care of our health. Ask your students to describe the different ways the people in the pictures are taking care of themselves. Then tell them that in this chapter of *Making a Difference* they will learn how to perform the mitzvah of *sh'mirat habriyut.*

### THINK ABOUT IT! (page 79)

Ask for a volunteer to read this feature aloud. How is Philo's point of view different from Hillel's? *(For Hillel, our body is sacred because it was created in God's image [see page 78 of the textbook]. For Philo, our body holds our soul, our link to God.)*

*Note:* Pronounce the "i" in Philo as *eye.*

### CARING FOR OURSELVES IS A RELIGIOUS DUTY (pages 79–81)

Depending on the comfort level of your students, you can either elicit personal responses to the questions that are posed in this section—for example, questions that ask how students might react to excitement or stress—or you can generalize and ask what reactions different people might have.

### MY CHANGING PALETTE (page 79)

To extend this activity, you can invite your students to draw a self-portrait using one or several of the colors they have used to describe themselves.

### SELF-PORTRAIT (page 80)

Invite your students to share what they have written, but remember that the main purpose of this activity is to help students consider how Jewish tradition and values can play a part in their growing sense of self and independence. Permit them to share what they have written, but respect their desire for privacy, if that is what they choose.

### READY! SET! GO! (pages 83–85)

As a class, read and discuss the suggestions for fulfilling the mitzvah of *sh'mirat habriyut.* Have students work individually, in small groups, or as a class to develop their ability to be more self-aware and to care for themselves. You also may want to invite an older teen, as a guest to do a presentation for them. For example, you might invite a teen who is a member of Students Against Drunk Driving (SADD).

### IT'S A DILEMMA! (page 86)

Students can work individually or in small groups to brainstorm solutions to the dilemma. Beyond soliciting responses to the dilemma, focus students on the religious obligation to take care of themselves and to reach deep inside to find the courage to withstand negative peer pressure. You may want to review Hillel's and Philo's views on why our bodies are sacred.

### A TIMELESS INTERNET (page 87)

Encourage students to share with the class what they wrote.

### MITZVAH JOURNAL (page 88)

The students can complete their journals at home or in class and then participate in a class discussion.

# Family Activity

Here is a sample letter to parents. Alternatively, you can create a special event for your students and their families. For example, invite a guest speaker to discuss substance abuse from a Jewish perspective. You can contact your local Federation for suggestions about speakers who have both the Jewish knowledge and background in teaching about substance abuse and how families can work together to avoid or overcome problems.

---

Dear Parent:

Our class has just studied the mitzvah of *sh'mirat habriyut*, caring for our physical and emotional health. Ask your child to explain why Judaism considers caring for our bodies and our emotional well-being a religious obligation.

As a family, discuss how you each currently perform the mitzvah of *sh'mirat habriyut*—for example, by getting adequate rest, brushing your teeth regularly, and reaching out to others when you feel ill or stressed. Then consider ways in which you can support each other to expand your observance of the mitzvah. For example, how might you help one another develop better eating habits? What exercise can you participate in as a family?

You might want to write a contract in which each of you commits to observing an act of *sh'mirat habriyut* beyond what you currently do and pledge to support each other in fulfilling your commitments. For example, one person might commit to exercising three times a week and the other members of the family could commit to helping that person make the time to do so.

If your family is comfortable with sharing its contract with our class, we would be pleased to have your child bring it in as a model for us.

Sincerely,
[Your name]

# Bikkur Ḥolim

## reach out and touch someone

Textbook pages 89–98

### SET INDUCTION

Play Debbie Friedman's song *"Mi Shebeirach."* The song is available on a number of CDs, including *Debbie Friedman at Carnegie Hall* (Sounds Write Productions, 1996). Alternatively, you can invite your cantor or music specialist to teach it to the class.

### LEARNING OBJECTIVES

Students will be able to:

• articulate the value of visiting the sick, *bikkur ḥolim,* as a sacred act

• discuss the fears and inhibitions that may discourage them from visiting the ill, and develop strategies to overcome these concerns

• perform acts of *bikkur ḥolim* that are meaningful to them and responsive to the needs of others

Tell your students that *mi shebeirach* means "May the One who blessed [our ancestors]," and explain that these words begin many prayers that ask God for a variety of blessings. For example, they are recited at bar and bat mitzvah celebrations when the rabbi asks God to bless and guide the teen through life. But they are most commonly recited as part of the prayer that asks God to help bring healing to the sick.

### KEY WORD

***Bikkur Ḥolim:*** visiting the sick

### CHAPTER OVERVIEW

In this chapter students will explore the concept of visiting the sick as a religious duty. They will develop skills to reduce their own discomfort in visiting someone who is critically ill or suffering from a debilitating disease, and they will learn how they can help bring comfort to the sick. Practical suggestions are provided for observing the mitzvah of *bikkur ḥolim.*

When you teach this chapter, be alert to your students. Some may be dealing with a loved one who suffers from a serious physical or mental illness and may therefore feel uncomfortable with the subject matter. If you are concerned about a pupil, you can contact your educational director, rabbi, or your synagogue's *Bikkur Ḥolim* Committee to find out if there is a problem. If there is, you can consult with the education director or the rabbi (or social worker, if your congregation has one) to discuss how you might best express your concern.

Review the lyrics of this song, and point out the words in the second verse: "renewal of body, renewal of spirit." Remind your students that Judaism teaches that we are God's partners in repairing the world. Say, "If that is true, who is responsible for helping God to renew the body of someone who is sick?" *(doctors, nurses, medical professionals)* "Who do you think is responsible for renewing a person's spirit?" *(rabbis, chaplains, priests, psychotherapists)* "Are professional health care specialists and clergy God's only partners in healing?" *(Allow responses.)* "In fact, Judaism teaches that we all are God's partners in this effort."

Ask: How does it feel to be obligated to help renew those who are ill? *(important, holy, scary, overwhelming)* Tell your students that in the next chapter of *Making a Difference* they will learn more about the mitzvah of *bikkur holim*, the sacred act of visiting the ill.

## OFFERING COMFORT AND HOPE (page 90)

Ask your students to think of a time when they were ill, perhaps with a cold, the flu, a tonsillectomy, or a broken leg. Then ask, "How did your family and friends respond?" *(brought presents, made chicken soup, sent cards, called, visited)* "How did their attention feel?" *(great, made me feel loved, reassuring, began to annoy me after a while)* "How might it have felt if no one had paid attention to you?" *(miserable, lonely, depressing, painful)*.

Now ask your students why they think that some people avoid visiting those who are ill, especially if they are in a hospital or nursing home suffering from a serious illness or injury. *(fear, awkwardness, embarrassment, discomfort)* Tell your students that they will now read about some of the reasons why people resist visiting those who are seriously ill. Have students take turns reading from "Understanding Our Fears" on pages 91–92 of the textbook.

## YOU DON'T SAY! (page 90)

Ask students to describe "a merry heart." *(happy, upbeat, positive in outlook)* What might be the benefit to being upbeat when you are sick? *(Many doctors believe that a positive outlook is an important element of healing.)* What about when you are the visitor? *(You can help renew the spirits of the person who is ill.)*

## UNDERSTANDING OUR FEARS (pages 91–92)

When you discuss this section of the chapter, be alert to the sensitivities of your students—some may be struggling with the issues it raises. Therefore, do not press students to participate in the discussion if they prefer not to. Reassure students that sending a card can be a valuable way to observe the mitzvah of *bikkur holim*.

## SELF-PORTRAIT (page 91)

Invite students to share their responses.

## READY! SET! GO! (pages 93–95)

Review "Understanding Our Fears" (pages 91–92) and "Check Your Priorities" (page 92). Ask your students if they can think of other reasons for feeling uncomfortable about visiting the sick. *(Seeing someone in a hospital bed is a reminder of a beloved friend or family member who died or is ailing.)* Ask: Why is it important to be aware of your reasons for wanting to avoid visiting the sick? *(The more we understand why we are uncomfortable, the easier it can be to address our concerns.)*

Hand out one sheet of paper to each student. Tell the students to make a chart by dividing the paper into three columns: "I Have Done This," "I Can Do This," and "This Looks Difficult." Then have them categorize the eight suggestions in the "Ready! Set! Go!" section by writing the boldface title of each in one of the three columns.

You may want to invite a *bikkur holim* specialist to your class. This person may be a member of the synagogue's *Bikkur Holim* Committee, a member of a community-wide committee, a clinical social worker from the local Jewish Family Service, or a member of the synagogue who is a clinical social worker. Share the "Ready! Set! Go!" exercise in advance with the specialist. Ask the person to talk with your students about their charts and offer guidance in some of the more difficult aspects of *bikkur holim*—for example, how to determine when to end a visit and how to determine when a patient would prefer to receive cards or a call rather than a visit.

As a follow-up to the visit by the specialist, ask your students to review their charts. Encourage them to update them if they now consider any of the suggestions more or less difficult. Then have your students implement one or two of the suggestions.

### THINK ABOUT IT! (page 96)

What do you think the visitor hoped to accomplish with her gift *(wanted to put the sick person in a positive frame of mind by helping her envision leaving the hospital and needing the raincoat)* Do you think it was a good idea? (***Yes:*** *It may have renewed the sick person's spirit and provided encouragement.* ***No:*** *It could have depressed the patient, who may have believed that he or she would be too ill to go outside.)*

### IT'S A DILEMMA! (page 96)

Do "It's a Dilemma!" as a 5-minute freeze-frame script. Ask for one volunteer to be the person who is ill and another to be the visitor. Invite the rest of the class to gather around the scene to help provide responses for the actors.

To begin the freeze-frame activity, encourage the "sick person" to behave in a grumpy and rude manner. Tell the "visitor" to make an effort not to become frustrated and walk out. At key moments, stop the action and ask the class to suggest responses or behaviors to the volunteers. (See "It's a Dilemma!" on page 27 of this teaching guide for a model of how this can be done.)

You might suggest that the patient reveal something personal during the conversation, such as an anxiety about increased pain or another fear that is related to his or her illness. Ask the students to consider this information when they suggest responses to the visitor.

After the freeze-frame activity, ask your students to complete "It's a Dilemma!" and invite them to share their responses.

### TEENS MAKE A DIFFERENCE (page 97)

Ask your students what kinds of problems they think Alan and Sharon Kohn may have encountered besides those that are mentioned in the book. *(anxious about kids becoming ill in the middle of the project, broke a hospital rule, had personality conflicts with a patient or member of the staff)* Write their responses on the chalkboard. After you have a list of six or seven items, ask students why it might be easier to deal with such problems if you were volunteering with a family member or friend.

### MITZVAH JOURNAL (page 98)

Students can complete their journals at home or in class and then participate in a class discussion.

---

## Family Activity

In place of a letter to your students' parents, you may want to organize a trip to a nursing home around the time of a Jewish holiday and invite your students and their families to participate in the event. Try to include an activity related to the holiday. For example, if you schedule the visit during Hanukkah, you can light Hanukkah candles and sing songs as part of your visit; if it is at the time of Tu B'Shevat, you may want to conduct a Tu B'Shevat seder.

---

# Kibbud Av Va'em

## the most difficult mitzvah?

Textbook pages 99–110

### TEACHING OPPORTUNITIES

#### SET INDUCTION

Ask your students to complete the following sentence silently, in their heads: The last time my parents made me angry or upset was because.... Now ask them to complete this statement silently as well: The last time I did something to demonstrate my respect for my parents was when I....

Now ask: Which of the two situations was easier to remember and why do you think that was so? After several minutes of discussion, tell your students that in the this chapter of *Making a Difference* they will explore the mitzvah of *kibbud av va'em*, the Jewish responsibility to honor one's parents.

### LEARNING OBJECTIVES

Students will be able to:

- understand the religious and spiritual duty to honor parents
- develop strategies for improving communications with their parents
- identify ways to honor their parents

### KEY WORDS

- **Kibbud Av Va'em:** honoring one's parents (literally, honoring one's father and mother)
- **Kibbud:** honor (how we act)
- **Yirah:** reverence (our attitude)

### CHAPTER OVERVIEW

As the subtitle of this chapter suggests, *kibbud av va'em* may be the most difficult mitzvah. Therefore, this chapter helps students explore the following concepts: As we mature, from children to adolescents to adults, we begin to pull away from our parents, to weigh their choices for us against our own choices. Of course, rebellion is part of adolescence. But Judaism teaches us to temper our rebellion and to treat our parents with honor and respect.

Once again, you may find that class discussions provoke strong feelings in some of your students, and perhaps even in you. At such times, it is especially important to create a safe learning environment in which feelings are heard, not judged.

## THEY GAVE US LIFE AND CONTINUE TO SUSTAIN US (page 100)

In consideration of the feelings of students who were adopted, you might point out that Jewish tradition regards those who raise a child as though they were the birth parents.

Ask your students to turn to the picture of the Ten Commandments on page 10 (English) or page 108 (Hebrew). Say: This is a representation of the Ten Commandments. Why do you think *kibbud av va'em*—honoring your parents—is one of the commandments, along with laws affirming God and prohibiting murder and theft? Allow the students to speculate, then ask: Why do you think there is no commandment to honor children—aren't children important? *(It is natural for parents to love their children and nurture them, but in the process of becoming independent, children may be tempted to ignore their parents or be disrespectful.)*

### Enrichment

Jewish tradition teaches that the first four commandments relate to our relationship to God and the second five to our relationship with one another. As the fifth commandment, the obligation to honor our parents is a bridge. Our parents are our link to God in the most fundamental way, and how we are taught to love and respect our parents has a critical impact on how we relate to everyone else in our lives.

## YOU DON'T SAY! (page 101)

Ask: Do you think *kibbud av va'em* is the hardest mitzvah? Harder than observing Shabbat? Kashrut? Why? *(**Yes:** It involves much more difficult emotional issues than what I eat or how I spend time. **No:** It is not as difficult as forming new habits regarding food and time.)*

### Photograph of Mother and Son (page 102)

Read the caption and invite your students to share situations in which their parents were trying to be helpful but your students felt pressured or resentful. Ask them how they handle such situations and how they communicate their feelings and preferences to their parents.

## SELF-PORTRAIT (pages 103–105)

Ask the students to complete the self-portraits. As an enrichment, you may want to ask them to write a letter of appreciation to one or both of their parents or guardians. The letters should be based on their self-portraits. Alternatively, you may offer students the option of writing a letter to the child they hope to have some day, expressing how they will try to earn their child's respect and how they want to be treated by him or her.

## READY! SET! GO! (pages 106–109)

Ask your students to read silently the suggestions for how to observe *kibbud av va'em*. Write the boldface headings for each of the five suggestions on the chalkboard and ask students for concrete ideas on how to implement the suggestions. Record their responses on the chalkboard. Suggest that they try to implement two to three of them.

You may also want to discuss if and how these suggestions can be applied to grandparents, teachers, coaches, and other adults.

### IT'S A DILEMMA! (page 109)

Divide the class into groups of two or three students. Ask them to discuss the dilemma, focusing on its two parts: As the son or daughter you have your own principles, but you also want to be respectful of your parent. After the groups have had an opportunity to brainstorm, bring the class back together and ask the groups to share their solutions.

Alternatively, you may want to organize this activity as a freeze-frame script. If you do, see "It's a Dilemma!" on pages 27 and 34 in this teaching guide for models.

### MITZVAH JOURNAL (page 110)

Students can complete their journals at home or in class and then participate in a class discussion.

## Family Activity

As an alternative to writing a letter, you may want to suggest to your synagogue that a regular or family Shabbat service be devoted to honoring parents. Ask your rabbi and cantor or music specialist for guidance in locating readings from sacred texts, such as Pirke Avot, and for songs that would be appropriate. You can also create a writing assignment for your class that results in readings for the occasion, for example, original poems or essays on parent-child relationships. Send out invitations to the families of the entire religious school and invite other classes to participate in selecting and creating readings.

# Sh'mirat Halashon

## weigh your words

Textbook pages 111–118

### LEARNING OBJECTIVES

Students will be able to:

- identify harmful language, *l'shon hara*
- articulate the reasons they may be tempted to speak ill of others
- describe one or more ways they can observe the mitzvah of guarding one's tongue, *sh'mirat halashon*

### KEY WORDS

- **L'shon Hara:** evil tongue; harmful language
- **Sh'mirat Halashon:** guarding one's tongue; watching one's speech

### CHAPTER OVERVIEW

Certain mitzvot, such as kashrut, present logistical difficulties: *Where* will I eat? *What* can I eat? *What if* my friend's home isn't kosher? In contrast, *sh'mirat halashon* is not a logistical mitzvah. It is a mitzvah that relies on our sensitivity to others and our ability to resist peer pressure. This chapter provides a religious and spiritual context for exploring what harmful speech is, including gossip and unkind remarks, and how it can be avoided.

### TEACHING OPPORTUNITIES

#### SET INDUCTION

Tell your class the following story, which is based on a hasidic tale.

Once there was a man who lived in a small village. He often talked about others without regard for the truth. Soon no one in the village wanted to speak with him.

Disheartened, the man went to his rabbi for help. The rabbi said, "Go home and rip open a pillow that is filled with feathers and bring it to me."

By the time the man brought the torn pillow to the rabbi, the wind had blown all the feathers away! "Now collect the feathers," the rabbi said.

"But they've blown away!" the man responded.

"So it is with what you say," the rabbi said. "Once words leave your mouth, you can never take them back."

Ask your students if words have ever "flown" out of their mouths that they later regretted because there was no way to take them back. Discuss several instances and how the students felt. Then tell your students that in this chapter of *Making a Difference* they will learn about the mitzvah of guarding one's tongue, *sh'mirat halashon.*

### A MATTER OF COURAGE (page 112)

After reading this section, ask your students to give examples of how positive peer pressure helps them find courage. *(friends encourage me to: believe in myself; stand up for what I think is right; not hang out with people who are put-down artists)* List their responses on the chalkboard. Then ask your students to try to integrate them in a role-playing or freeze-frame activity in which several students are gossiping about a new student in their class.

### THINK ABOUT IT! (page 112)

Discuss possible interpretations of the proverb. *(Literal meaning: A person might die because of what is said—for example, because of false testimony—while a word can restore a person's life—for example, a government pardon. Symbolic interpretations: a friendship can die because of unkind words or lies, or it can blossom because of empathetic or patient words.)*

### ANCIENT TEACHINGS FOR MODERN LIFE (page 113)

Here is the transliteration of the Hebrew in this exercise:

*Lo tisa sheima shav...*
*Lo tekaleil heireish...*
*Lo teileich rachil be'amecha.*

Ask: Why do you think there is a specific prohibition against insulting the deaf? *(They can't hear and thus cannot defend themselves.)* Do you think the Torah is referring only to the deaf or hearing impaired? Who else might not be able to hear? *(someone who is not present when the words are spoken, someone who doesn't speak the language, someone who doesn't understand what is being said because the point is made subtly)*

### READY! SET! GO! (pages 114–116)

Divide students into groups of two and three. Depending on your class size, assign each group to one or two of the suggestions in this section. Then have the group read the suggestions and discuss (1) whether or not they think these are realistic approaches and why, and (2) whether or not they think following these suggestions would help them become the adults they want to become and why. Ask each group to assign a recorder to take notes and report back to the class.

Reassemble the class and ask the recorder of each group to summarize their discussion. Ask the students to select two or three suggestions from "Ready! Set! Go!" and apply them to their lives. Remind your students that to commit to observing a mitzvah is not to be perfect, but rather to strive to improve yourself.

### YOU DON'T SAY! (page 116)

Ask students to respond to this question. *(If you hear someone lying and you do not speak up, others might assume that the statements are true. If you hear someone calling out names or racial epithets and you remain silent, it is as if you agree.)*

### THINK ABOUT IT! (page 116)

Discuss the idea that people who put others down are "advertising" that they don't feel good about themselves.

### IT'S A DILEMMA! (page 116)

Ask students to complete the activity individually or in small collaborative learning groups, then conduct a class discussion. Encourage the students to consider many possibilities when responding to the dilemma. *(Silence might indicate that you agree with your friends' assessment of the situation. Changing the subject could be helpful but might still leave a negative impression about your friend. If you defend your friend by sharing his personal situation, you run the risk of breaching his confidence. If you suggest that he may be distracted by personal concerns and that he just needs some time, you may help the others be less judgmental.)*

### SELF-PORTRAIT (page 117)

Have students complete and share their responses in class. You may want to explore your students' attitudes toward deprecating humor in light of the "Think About It!" activity on page 116. Ask: Is it *l'shon hara* to laugh at someone else's expense? *(Any time we joke about someone else, we are using words to harm.)* If you discuss political humor, you may want to focus on the difference between jokes that are said for a mean or hurtful purpose versus those that are meant to help us question the status quo or view a person or situation in a different or more thoughtful way.

### MITZVAH JOURNAL (page 118)

Students can complete their journals at home or in class and then participate in a class discussion.

# Family Activity

Here is a sample letter.

---

Dear Parent:

We have just completed a unit on the mitzvah of *sh'mirat halashon*, guarding one's tongue. We explored Jewish perspectives on hurtful speech, bearing tales, gossiping, and breaching confidentiality. A key term your child learned is *l'shon hara* (literally, "the evil tongue"), which is a derogatory or damaging statement that is said for a mean or hurtful purpose. We discussed a number of strategies for improving the way we treat others by choosing the words we use.

One point we focused on is that confident, secure people don't need to belittle others and that putting others down can be an "advertisement" for one's own insecurities or self-contempt. You might discuss this idea over dinner and consider how to work as a family to make your home a put-down-free environment.

Sincerely,

[Your name]

# ⑬ Tefillah

## an open line

Textbook pages 119–129

### LEARNING OBJECTIVES

Students will be able to:

- understand how prayer can strengthen them and connect them to the Jewish community
- expand the role of prayer in their lives in ways that are personally and communally meaningful

### KEY WORD

*Tefillah:* prayer

### CHAPTER OVERVIEW

In this chapter students will explore prayer as a means of talking with God and connecting to Jewish communities around the world and across time. They also will learn how prayer helps us express deep feelings, such as gratitude, fear, and joy. The chapter offers practical suggestions on how to increase the opportunities to observe the mitzvah of prayer, or *tefillah*.

**SET INDUCTION**

Ask your students if they ever talk to God. What subjects or concerns do they talk about? How do they feel when they talk to God? How do they feel afterwards? *(stronger, safer, loved, calmer)* Ask your students if they can think of another word for talking to God. *(praying)*

Select a short prayer, such as the Sh'ma, and recite it together as a class. Then ask the students to recite the same prayer to themselves. Is that experience different? (If yes, ask students to describe the difference.)

Tell your students that they will be exploring the different types and purposes of prayer, *tefillah*, in this chapter of *Making a Difference*.

## SACRED FOOTPRINTS (page 120)

Read this section and ask your students to describe situations in which they have experienced God's presence or a feeling of holiness. *(holding a baby, seeing a snow-covered mountain or a sunset, smelling a rose garden)* Ask them to describe times when they have felt a holy presence while praying or standing in the synagogue. *(when they have recited a silent prayer from the heart, during Kol Nidre on Yom Kippur, when they held a Torah scroll or opened the Holy Ark)*

## LETTING GOD IN (page 120)

Resources and space permitting, you may want to provide large sheets of paper for this activity, so that the results can be posted on your bulletin board.

## YOU DON'T SAY! (page 121)

After students complete this writing activity, invite them to share their responses. *(One response might be that sometimes we focus only on what we don't have. Saying a blessing reminds us of what we do have.)*

## PRAYER CAN HELP US SORT OUT OUR EMOTIONS (page 122)

After reading this section, ask your students, "How can *tefillah* help you sort out your feelings? How can it help you arrive at a clearer understanding of what you want or need?"

## YOU ARE NOT ALONE (page 123)

After reading this section, ask your students, "How can *tefillah* help you feel connected to the Jewish community? How can it prevent you from becoming self-centered?"

## SELF-PORTRAIT (page 124)

After your students complete their self-portrait, ask them to consider the following question: What part of the synagogue service would they feel most comfortable leading and why? You may want to invite your cantor or a teen who leads your Junior Congregation to speak to the class about the challenges and rewards of leading services.

## READY! SET! GO! (pages 125–127)

As a class, read and discuss the suggestions on these pages. Ask students to consider which suggestions are most practical, interesting, or motivating for them to implement. (Point out that, like other mitzvot, the mitzvah of *tefillah* is not an all-or-nothing commitment.)

Ask your students to think about which suggestions they can add to their weekly or monthly routines and which would be more occasional activities for them. Have them choose one or more suggestions to implement.

## IT'S A DILEMMA! (page 128)

Divide your class into collaborative learning groups of two or three students and ask them to brainstorm responses. After five or ten minutes, ask each group to report their solutions to the class. *(stop praying aloud and stand or sit silently; walk out so that no one sees how upset you are; stop praying aloud, but find comfort by silently reciting other prayers that are found in the siddur or are from the heart)*

## MITZVAH JOURNAL (page 129)

Students can complete their journals at home or in class and then participate in a class discussion.

# Family Activity

Here is a sample letter.

Dear Parent:

We have completed our unit on Jewish traditions of prayer, or *tefillah*. Our class has discussed personal versus communal prayer, and how each can be of help to us.

One important purpose of prayer is to focus us on the good in our lives. The *Sheheḥeyanu* blessing does exactly that. It is a Jewish tradition to celebrate the start of Jewish holidays, first-time events—such as the first time you drive a car, wear a pair of sneakers, get an A during a semester— and other joyous occasions—such as birthdays, graduations, weddings, and anniversaries—by reciting this blessing.

Here are the words:
*Baruch atah adonai eloheinu melech ha' olam, sheheḥeyanu, vekiyemanu vehigiyanu laz' man hazeh.* (Blessed are You, Adonai our God, Ruler of the universe, who has given us life, sustained us, and brought us to this moment.)

You may want to recite this blessing as a family at celebratory moments, both large and small. You also may want to create a "Family Book of Celebrations" in which you record these moments.

Sincerely,

[Your name]

# 14 Talmud Torah

## learning matters

Textbook pages 130–138

### LEARNING OBJECTIVES

Students will be able to:

- articulate the importance of continuing one's Jewish education as a mitzvah
- develop a plan for continuing their Jewish learning

### KEY WORD

**Talmud Torah:** the study of Torah; also, Jewish learning in the broadest sense

### CHAPTER OVERVIEW

This chapter focuses on the mitzvah of Torah study, in particular the importance of continued participation in Jewish learning and communal life. Students will encounter a variety of options for pursuing a lifelong involvement with Jewish education and the Jewish community.

### TEACHING OPPORTUNITIES

#### SET INDUCTION

Draw a large outline of a tree on the chalkboard. Say to your students, "The Torah is often referred to as *Etz Ḥayyim*, The Tree of Life. What does that expression mean?" *(It keeps our people alive.)* "Let's list some of the ways the Torah keeps the Jewish people alive." You may want to suggest that students think about the mitzvot they have studied. *(The laws of the Torah teach us how to live; the Torah connects us to the Source of Life, God; it guides us toward healthy behaviors* [sh'mirat habriyut]*; it teaches us to be God's partners in renewing others* [bikkur holim] *and in renewing the Earth's resources* [bal tashḥit]*.)*

Write each response on the chalkboard and draw a fruit around it so that when you have six or seven responses the tree looks like a fruit tree. Say to your students, "Like a fruit tree, the Torah offers us sustenance each day, day after day, week after week, year after year. In this chapter of *Making a Difference*, you will find out how to be nurtured continually by Torah by being involved with Jewish learning throughout your life."

Read the introduction to the chapter and, with your students, discuss the questions it raises.

### THINK ABOUT IT! (page 131)

Before your class answers these questions, lead a discussion on how your students could benefit from continuing to study the mitzvot presented in *Making a Difference*. For example, how might their perspective on kashrut, observing Shabbat, *kibbud av va'em*, or *sh'mirat habriyut* change when they are adults? How might continuing to study these and other Jewish issues when they are older deepen their understanding of Judaism and better equip them to live life more fully, more healthfully, and with more meaning?

### IT'S A DILEMMA! (page 132)

Pose this question to the class and ask for other examples besides basketball practice. *(choir, dance class, etc.)* Ask how students would solve the problem. Point out that first, they have to agree that *both* activities are desirable. They have to want to continue study as much as they want the extracurricular activity.

Some solutions involve the wording of "same day." What does that mean? Are both activities at the same time? Or is the school activity right after school? Many teen education programs are in the evening. Might they attend both? Could they get permission from their education program to come in late, directly from practice? Might there be another program in the community that would not conflict with their sports program? Is there another sport activity that would not conflict with their education program?

### YOU DON'T SAY! (page 133)

What did Ben Bag Bag mean? *(As we grow and mature, we gain new insights from texts we have studied previously.)*

### SELF-PORTRAIT (page 134)

After your students complete their self-portraits, take a poll to find out who is interested in Jewish activities. Who is interested in leading Junior Congregation? In going to a Jewish museum? In doing Israeli dancing? Then ask: How would you go about doing this? What are the community's resources? (You may want to bring in several local Jewish newspapers so that your students can look through them and find the kinds of community activities in which they expressed an interest.)

### TEENS MAKE A DIFFERENCE (page 135)

Ask your students: Must you go to Havana to make a difference? How else might you affect Jews who are not connected with the Jewish community or who have expressed a desire to learn more about Judaism? *(work on tzedakah projects that target Jewish immigrants; offer to tutor an adult who wants to learn Hebrew; invite a Jewish friend who is not actively involved in Jewish life to attend synagogue services with you or to join you and your family for Shabbat dinner)*

### READY! SET! GO! (pages 136–137)

As a class, read and discuss the suggestions on these pages. Ask the students to consider which suggestions are most practical, interesting, or motivating for them to implement.

Ask your students to think about which suggestions they can add to their weekly or monthly routines and which would be more occasional activities for them. Have your students choose one or more suggestions to implement.

**MITZVAH JOURNAL** (page 138)

Students can complete their journals at home or in class and then participate in a class discussion.

## Family Activity

As an alternative to a letter, you may want to invite your students and their families to a special event at your synagogue. For example, you might invite them to spend time in your synagogue's library and encourage them to borrow a book, video, or musical recording. Also invite them to browse through the Jewish newspapers and magazines. Make the occasion festive: Serve food and perhaps invite your cantor or music specialist to teach some Israeli music, or show an Israeli feature film with subtitles.

# ⑮ Going Forward

Bring matches and enough Shabbat candles to class so that you can give one to each student and have one for yourself. Hand out the candles and set the matches aside. Darken the room by closing the shades and turning off the lights.

## BEGIN THE CLASS BY TELLING THE FOLLOWING STORY:

One day the students of a learned rabbi asked him how to rid the world of evil and injustice. "Tell us how to remove this darkness from the Earth," they begged.

"Let us seek the answer in the cellar," the rabbi said.

He handed every student a candle and led them down the wooden stairs. The students wondered why their teacher was taking them to such a dark and cold place.

Then the rabbi lit his own candle. It was still dark. But when he used his candle to light everyone else's, the basement was filled with light.

Then the rabbi explained, "Do not despair over evil and injustice. Instead, work together to remove it from God's world. Just as God brought light into the world through Creation, so we can bring light through the mitzvot we perform."

Ask your students: What does light symbolize in this story? *(hope, wisdom, goodness)* Ask: How can the mitzvah of tzedakah add light to the world? How can *tefillah? rodef shalom? talmud Torah?*

Call on students to read pages 139 to 140, stopping at the next to the last paragraph, which begins, "May your life...." At that point, light your candle and, as you read the final two paragraphs to your students, one by one, light their candles. When you have finished, you may want to lead your students in a closing song, such as *"Oseh Shalom."* Ask your students to blow out their candles and to save them as a keepsake to remind them that they have the power and the responsibility to add light to the world.

# Working with Students with Special Needs

Like most classes, yours probably includes a diverse group of students. Some may require extra attention to succeed. The activities in this guide are intended for a wide variety of learners and therefore employ a variety of modalities. There are opportunities for written as well as oral expression, visual as well as verbal activities. There is collaborative learning as well as individual work, and most activities can be adapted to accommodate special learners.

For students with special learning needs, consider using one or several of these strategies:

• Mask parts of the textbook page so that only the activity being taught is visible.

• Highlight the information in the text to which students should pay especially close attention.

• Help students to share what they know in ways that are compatible with their learning styles. For example, where appropriate, allow students to answer questions orally instead of writing their answers.

• Paraphrase and summarize what has been taught. This is helpful for all students.

• Provide students with special learning needs extra time to finish assignments, or reduce the number of items they are expected to complete.

• Repeat new words and concepts a number of times. Do not assume that students with special needs will recognize them when they see or hear them again later in the class session or the following week.

• If students have difficulty pronouncing the Hebrew vocabulary, model the words for them and have them repeat the words after you.

• Set all your students up for success. When assigning students to small groups, be sure students with special needs can make a contribution to the group. If they cannot, either choose a different class assignment or provide an alternative learning experience for the students with special learning needs.

• Ask for guidance from your educational director.

Most important, remember that the interpersonal relationships you build and the tone and atmosphere you create in your classroom are as important as the material you teach. Try to be relaxed, respectful, and patient with students who have learning challenges. Model the kind of Jewish behaviors that you are teaching through the mitzvot. And finally, try to encourage patience and tolerance in all of your students.